not a guide to
Manchester

Ben McGarr

First published 2012

The History Press
97 St George's Place,
Cheltenham, Gloucestershire, GL50 3QB
www.thehistorypress.co.uk

British Library Cataloguing in Publication Data.
A catalogue record for this book is available from the British Library.

ISBN 978 0 7524 7119 8

Typesetting and origination by The History Press
Printed by TJ International Ltd, Padstow, Cornwall

Coat of Arms

The shield is taken from the arms of the Norman barons of Manchester, the Grelleys, and topped with a reference to the Manchester Ship Canal that made our inland city a seaport.

*

The crest is crowned by a globe, signifying the scale of Manchester trade. It is covered by bees – an allusion to our industry.

*

The supporters are each emblazoned with a red rose of Lancaster, as a nod to the county in which the town emerged.

*

The gold chain of the antelope refers to our engineering, and the castellated crown of the lion refers to the original Roman fort from which Manchester grew.

*

The Motto is *Concilio et Labore*, 'By counsel and hard graft'.

Contents

Manchester

Pronounced /ˈmæntʃɛstə/ or rather /ˈmɒntʃɛstə/ by its inhabitants.

Alternatively, just 'Town'. (I myself had almost reached my second decade by the time I knew it as anything but the latter...)

Back-formation from the mediaeval forms and some speculative playing around with garbled Classical versions give us the original Latin *Mamucium*, a Romanisation of a Celtic place-name. Seemingly based on the root 'Mama', as in 'mammary gland', our settlement started out as 'Boob-place', referring to some breast-like shape evident in the local topography – probably the hill now occupied by the cathedral, though the original profile has long since been obscured.

When English speakers first arrived here in the seventh century AD, the local Romano-Britons had ground the Latin down into something like *Mamigi*. Left to its own devices, this might have ended up as Welsh *Mefyg*, but it was taken up by the Angles as *Mame* and fastened to their ending *-ceaster*, from the Latin word *castrum* or 'fort', which they used for old Roman ruins.

Mameceaster became Mamchester and finally, for ease's sake, Manchester.

Grid Reference

Ancient Manorial Hall – 53°48'6.54' N, 2° 24' 4.06' W

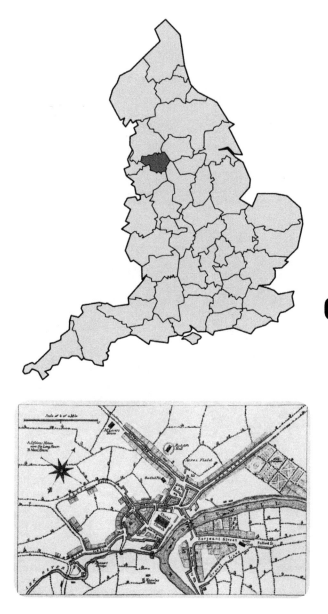

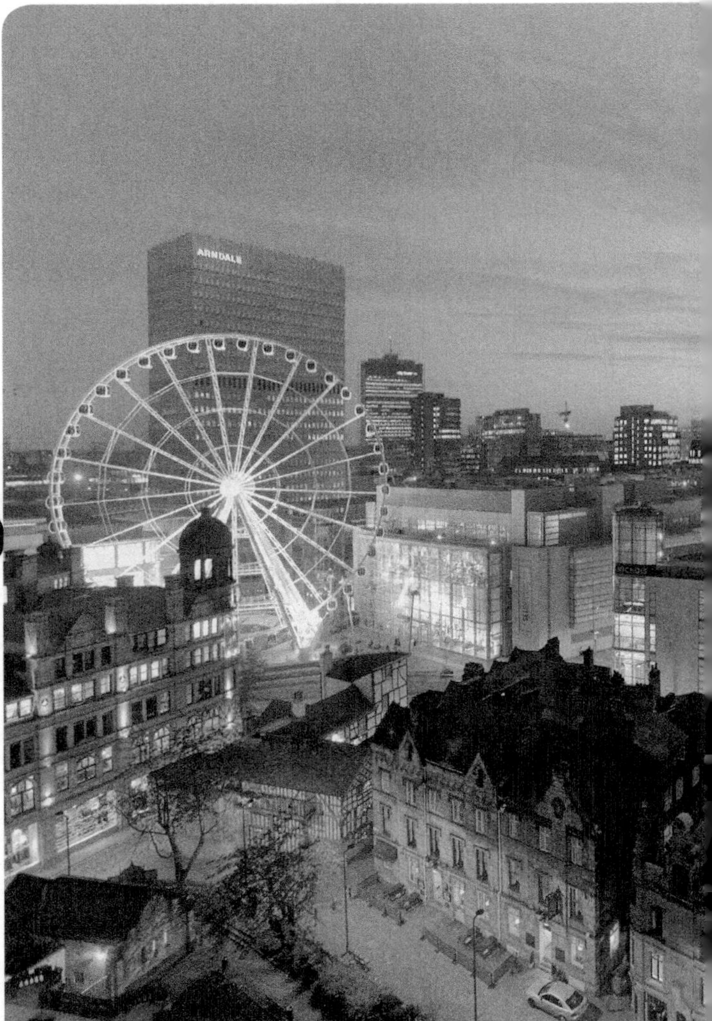
ARNDALE

Street Names

Most are Victorian memorials of long-forgotten civic worthies, but some are older and have curious origins.

Deansgate – The main north-south thoroughfare of the city, ending in the Norse 'gate' (like many old urban streets in Northern England). Formerly 'Denesgate', the name refers not to the ecclesiastical office, but to a now lost dene or gully which the street led to.

Hanging Ditch – A street following the old mediaeval defences of the 'citadel' formed by the Owd Church and the former castle. These took the form of a steep-sided cutting, described as 'hanging'. Whether the collection of refuse in the bottom of this made the ditch 'hanging' in the modern dialect sense (see 'Local Lingo') is unknown.

Fennel Street – Not from the herb, but from *vennel*, dialect for 'narrow lane'.

Walkers Croft – Now a small winding alley, this commemorates the former wide area of fullers' pits by the River Irk, where cloth was treated in a noxious urine-based mixture by workers known as 'walkers', thanks to their unenviable task of treading the liquid into the material.

Long Millgate – Site of the former watermill, powered by the Irk, to which townsfolk were forced to bring their grain, and pay the local baron for the privilege.

Shudehill – Obscure, but perhaps a dialect word for grain husks, hinting at the importance of this part of town as a distribution point for foodstuffs. My own great grandparents imported seed from dealers based here, all the way to Tipperary. It is, of course, a long way…

Alport Lane – Now the southern part of Deansgate, *Ald Port* is an Old English term for 'old town', indicating an early nucleus of settlement here by the old Roman fort, prior to the refocusing on the confluence of the Irk and Irwell.

Todd Street – Once the more picturesque Toad Lane, presumably for its damp nature, or else from T'Owd Lane, 'the old lane'.

Tib Street and Lane – Named after a long-lost rivulet, a modest cousin of the famous Tiber.

Withy Grove – Evidently rather greener in the past, when withies or willows still grew here.

Cateaton Street – Very obscure, but of doubtless antiquity. Older forms like 'Cattenelane' may employ some form of a now lost Old English *catte*, possibly referring to the defensive ditch once found here.

Bearings

In degrees from north, starting from the fountains in Piccadilly Gardens:

	Deg.	Distance
Cathedral	315	720 yards
MEN Arena	330	999 yards
Affleck's Palace	20	185 yards
Sport City	85	2,640 /1.5 miles
Piccadilly Station	138	620 yards
The Village	180	520 yards
University	181	1330 yards
Chinese Arch	210	396 yards
Roman Gatehouse	240	1,409 yards
Town Hall	245	565 yards
Arndale Shopping Centre	300	404 yards

Where Does Manchester Begin & End?

Not quite so simple a question. Like the Danube to Buda and Pest, the Irwell is the watery frontier between the two cities of Salford and Manchester. Salfordians might object to being referred to as Mancs, but they are unlikely to get a 'Not a Guide To' book of their own. And yet, the old mediaeval parish of Manchester included Salford, extending southward to the Mersey and eastward to Droylsden. Salford gets its own back, in that this parish was located in the Hundred of Salford, once known as Salfordshire. In 1974, 1,000 year-old counties were swept aside by bureaucratic decree, so that many young Mancs are ignorant of what Hundred they were born in. Many aren't even aware that they are Lancastrians.

The 'Metropolitan County of Greater Manchester' brought some recognition of the new industrial conurbation, but has since been chopped into ten smaller administrative units. Official 'Manchester' today is but one of these, forming a strange strip of land stretching from the city proper down into Cheshire and the airport. This has made our city seem deceptively small in statistics tables, with townships such as my own Failsworth (always identifying as Mancunian) annexed to the outer satellite towns. Cultural Manchester thus extends beyond the political boundaries.

For more utilitarian purposes, the Eurocrats have resurrected Greater Manchester as a 'Large Urban Zone'. Covering 2,007 square miles, and home to 2.6 million people, we are the seventeenth most populous 'LUZ' in the EU, and second in the UK after London.

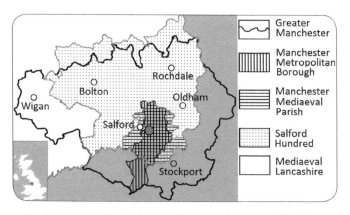

Greater Manchester

Manchester Metropolitan Borough

Manchester Mediaeval Parish

Salford Hundred

Mediaeval Lancashire

Wigan
Bolton
Rochdale
Oldham
Salford
Stockport

Distance From...

Place	Miles	Km
Ayers Rock, Australia	9,356	15,057
Brussels, Belgium	334	538
Centre of the Earth	3,975	6,397
Death Valley, USA	5,129	8,255
Eiffel Tower, Paris	375	604
Frankfurt, Germany	522	841
Glasgow, Scotland	183	295
Hong Kong, China	5,983	9,629
Istanbul, Turkey	1,683	2,709
The Kremlin, Russia	1,585	2,551
Lima, Peru	6,271	10,092
The Moon (average distance)	238,857	384,403
Niagara Falls, North America	3,438	5,532
Osaka, Japan	5,855	9,422
Panama Canal, Republic of Panama	5,198	8,366
Queenstown, New Zealand	11,720	18,861
Reykjavik, Iceland	1,012	1,629
Syracuse, Sicily	1,412	2,272
The Taj Mahal, India	4,350	7,001
Ural Mountains, Russia	2,215	3,565
Vatican City	1,050	1,689
Washington DC, USA	3,549	5,712
Xanthi, Greece	1,519	2,445
Yellowstone National Park, USA	4,465	7,186
Zurich, Switzerland	636	1,024

International Bearings

There are no fewer than thirty-two Manchesters in the USA, of which the most notable is the largest town in New Hampshire. Known as 'Derryfield' before 1810, Manchester NH emulated the manufacturing success of its namesake. It now has a population of 110,000 and has been rated by *Forbes* magazine as the 'cheapest place to live in the US'. A lot quieter than our town, it is ironically referred to as Manch Vegas.

'Manchester' became a byword for intense industrialisation, and so there are a host of unofficial 'Manchesters' around the world:

Mulhouse in France

India's Ahmedabad, 'the Manchester of the East'

Finnish Tampere – nicknamed 'Manse'

Brno, Grodno, Lodz and Covilhã are the Manchesters of Moravia, Belarus, Poland and Portugal, respectively.

In addition, several HMS *Manchesters* have sailed the briny main, and the *Manchester Bomber* was the immediate ancestor of the more famous *Lancaster*. The Manchester Regiment has been amalgamated with the Liverpool King's Regiment since 1958. Our one-time verminous slums were also the original home of the Manchester Terrier, a renowned 'ratter', and oldest recorded (1570) breed of terrier. The present 13th Earl of Manchester is an Australian-born American citizen living in California.

Town Twinnings

There have been many, but the street signs on Oldham Road have long proclaimed Russia's Saint Petersburg as our chief twin. While our town hasn't witnessed quite the tumultuous events that Petrograd did in the Revolutions of 1905 and 1917, or Leningrad in the grim 1940s German Blockade, both cities are the 'Northern Capital' of their countries.

Russian influence as yet amounts to only a trickle of individuals and the delightfully authentic 'Saint Petersburg' restaurant on Sackville Street, but who knows what oligarchs may take a shine to the place as time goes on...

Other twinned towns include:
Leningrad, USSR (1962), re-renamed 'Sankt Peterburg', Russia

Kanpur, India (1970)

Karl-Marx-Stadt, DDR (1983), now Chemnitz once more, in the reunited Germany

Wuhan, China (1986)

Faisalabad, Pakistan (1997)

Los Angeles, USA (2009)

Freak Weather

A never-before seen full day of unbroken sunshine was reported by scientists in...

... Well, no. Nothing too drastic to report here, as the chief feature of the town's micro-climate is the rather monotonous damp. This once did us a good turn, in so far as the very lack of changeability in the weather provided local entrepreneurs with the ideal conditions for processing cotton; preventing fires and thread breakage.

That said, recent years have brought some extremes. The unaccustomedly cold winter of 2010 resulted in business losses of £24 million for the January day when a foot of snow fell overnight. Things got so bad that *Coronation Street* was forced to cancel filming for the first time in fifteen years.

The year 2011 broke records too, with its 'Indian Summer' high of 28ºC on the first of October. Much of the present book was written in the more reassuringly familiar drizzle that filled the remainder of that month, however...

Average annual humidity: 86.3 per cent

Average annual rainfall: 31.8in

Rainy days per year: 140

Manchester lies in the middle of the Mersey basin, but flooding is more an issue of the distant past now that most local streams have been culverted out of sight. The Irk was once something of a rogue, however, with Mrs Banks' novel *A Manchester Man* describing a deluge in 1799. The Medlock has also misbehaved: in 1872, its torrents washed coffins and bodies down into the city from Philips Park Cemetery...

Timeline

King Aethelfrith's Angles invade; English first spoken here.

Norman Conquest; Manchester allotted to the Grelley family.

Charles Worsley takes seat as first Manchester Member of Parliament.

Roman Governor Gnaeus Julius Agricola conquers the Mersey basin, building the fort of Mamucium

Danish Conquest of the North. Flixton, Hulme and Urmston still retain their Danish names.

Town Charter granted by Thomas, 8th Baron Grelley.

Cloth industry is booming.

Pure cotton fabrics in production.

| AD 79 | c. 613 | 866 | 1066 | 1301 | 1500 | 1654 | 1750 |

| c.500 | 650 | 923 | 1250 | 1397 | 1642 | 1745 |

King Osweo rejoins us with the Kingdom of Northumbria.

Dyeing industry already in action.

Manchester unsuccessfully besieged by Royalists.

Bonnie Prince Charlie parades through the town, to the delight of th local Jacobit faction.

Lancelot's fabled struggle with the giant Tarquin of Manchester.

West Saxon King Edward the Elder defeats the Danes, joining Manchester to the Mercian Bishopric of Lichfield.

Baron (and priest) Thomas la Warre founds college for clergy (now Chetham's Library).

Cobden and Bright found the Anti-Corn Law League to campaign for Free Trade and cheaper bread.

Continuing redevelopment sees Manchester oust Birmingham as England's 'second city'.

Cromwell statue erected in front of the cathedral.

The devastating Christmas Blitz.

BBC occupy new headquarters at quayside MediaCity-UK.

The Bridgewater Canal is opened.

Granted City status.

Manchester Ship Canal opened.

The port is closed.

| 1761 | 1838 | 1853 | 1875 | 1894 | 1942 | 1982 | 2000 | 2011 |

| 1757 | 1819 | 1845 | 1868 | 1889 | 1931 | 1968 | 1996 | 2006 |

The 'Shude Hill Fight' – rioting over high food prices.

Irish Famine bolsters already pre-existing Irish community.

Manchester given County Borough status.

Royal Exchange closes down. Cromwell statue moved to Wythenshawe.

Common-wealth Games held at the new Sport City complex.

27

'Peterloo' – a massacre of peaceful protestors demanding political and social reform.

First Trade Union Congress held at the Mechanics' Institute.

Population peaks at 766,311.

IRA terrorists plant largest ever mainland bomb on Corporation Street.

A Day in the Life of Manchester

0500: Clubbers go home (or at least end up in somebody's home).

0600: Students of the country's biggest university finish essays after an all-nighter to meet today's deadline.

0730: Traffic begins to flow.

0800: The Mancunian Way viaduct is clogged.

0900: Workers spill out of the Metrolink trams.

1000: Shoppers trickle into the city centre.

1100: The city's day is in full swing.

1200: Piccadilly Gardens and other open spaces swell with lunching office workers.

1345: Budding musicians at Chetham's School of Music begin their daily free lunchtime concert.

1600: Traffic begins its flow out of the city as early leavers decide to pack it in for the day.

1700: Bus, tram and train systems straining at their peak.

1800: Later leavers swap the office for pubs and cafés.

1900: Few free tables remain at restaurants of all imaginable varieties.

1945: Evening kick off at the stadiums.

2100: Queues form at night clubs, and the red carpet of the Beetham Tower's lofty Cloud 23 bar fills with the 'in-crowd' and the wannabes.

0100-0400: Takeaways rake in their nightly profits.

How Many Times a Year...

20 million passengers and 150,000 tons of cargo on over 200,000 flights pass through Manchester Airport.

15,000,000+ tourists flock to Manchester, including 900,000 from overseas, supporting some 40,000 jobs.

Combined home-game crowds for the two Mancunian Premiership football clubs alone (never mind those of other divisions with their own loyal fans) put around 7,200,000 bums on seats in the world's Capital of Football.

The MEN Arena, biggest indoor arena in Europe and busiest arena venue in the world (2007 figures), holds over 250 events, seeing well over 1.5 million people pass through its doors.

Manchester Central Convention Complex (formerly GMEX) hosts several political party conferences and, with other venues, holds over twenty international conferences, and around a third of all other UK conventions.

Around 38 million shoppers visit the inner city Arndale Centre, and 35 million the out of town Trafford Centre.

Combined parades – Saint Pat's, Manchester Day, Manchester Pride – total around 230,000 people teeming through our streets.

Demographics

	Manchester	Greater Manchester
Population:	392,819	2,547,700
Men:	191,570	
Women:	201,249	

Ethnicity

'White':	318,013 or 81 per cent	91 per cent
	(of which 292,498 are 'British', 14,826 'Irish', and 10,689 'other')	
'Asian':	35,877 or 9 per cent	5.7 per cent
'Black':	17,739 or 4.5 per cent	1.2 per cent
Chinese/'Other':	8,517 or 2.3 per cent	
'Mixed':	12,673 or 3.2 per cent	
Foreign born:	15 per cent	7.2 per cent

Religion

Christian:	62.4 per cent	74 per cent
Muslim:	9.1 per cent	5 per cent
No religion:	16 per cent	11.4 per cent

Employment

Working:	46.4 per cent	
Unemployed:	3.5 per cent	
Under 24:	41.9 per cent	
Over 75:	6.4 per cent	7 per cent

(From the 2001 census)

Immigration since will have increased the foreign-born percentages, Eastern European and African particularly.

Smaller communities include around 25,000 Italians, enough Armenians to keep the Holy Trinity Armenian Apostolic Church going (oldest in the UK, founded 1870) and roughly 35,000 Jews.

Facts, Firsts & Lasts

The year 1761 saw the opening of the world's first commercial canal, named after its owner, the Duke of Bridgewater.

In 1830, the first passenger railway, from Liverpool to Manchester, was opened by the Duke of Wellington.

First cotton mill founded by Arkwright in 1780; Victorian 'Cottonopolis' manufactured 80 per cent of the world's cotton.

Manchester's Hallé Orchestra was founded in 1858, the oldest in Britain.

The world's first professional football league was set up in 1888, at the Royal Hotel in Piccadilly Square.

In 1896, Trafford Park became the world's first purpose-built industrial estate.

Manchester gave birth in 1809 to modern vegetarianism, inspired by Salford preacher William Cowherd.

Rolls first met Royce at the Midland Hotel in 1904.

In 1948, at the university, Kilburn and Williams' 'Baby' was the first computer to store a programme.

Manchester is home to the biggest and the wealthiest football club in the world. Oddly enough, they are not the same one!

Rivets from Park Bridge Ironworks between Oldham and Ashton held together both the *Titanic* and the Eiffel Tower.

Strangeways Prison saw (simultaneously with Liverpool's Walton Prison) the last execution by hanging at 8 a.m. on 13 August 1964.

Literary Quotations

'What Manchester says today, the rest of England says tomorrow.'

Oxford Dictionary of Proverbs

AD 923. This year King Edward… ordered another army… to go to Mameceaster in Northumbria, to repair and to man it. *65* Mancestre … is the fairest, best buildied, quikkest and most populus Tounne of al Lancastreshire.'

John Leland, *Itinerary*, 1538

'[Manchester] farre excelleth the townes lying round about it for the beautifull shew it carieth, for resort unto it, and for clothing, in regard also of the mercate place, the faire Church, and College… But in the foregoing age this towne was of farre greater account both for certain wollen clothes there wrought and in great request, commonly called Manchester Cottons… where the brooke Medlocke entreth into Irwell, I saw the plot and ground worke of an ancient Fortresse built foure square, commonly called Mancastle … the Fort of Mancunium and station of the Romans where they kept watch and ward.'

William Camden, *Britannia*, 1610

'Manchester is large, opulent, well-built. The women are esteemed handsome. Manchester is the best regulated town in England.'

Percival Barlow, *General History of Europe*, 1770

'The dress of the people here savors not much of the London mode in general; the people are remarkable for coarseness of feature, and the language is unintelligible.'

Samuel Curwen, *American Loyalist*, 1777

'If I should be so blessed as to revisit again my own country, but more especially Manchester, all that I could hope or desire would be presented before me in one view.'

Robert Clive (Clive of India), late 1700s

Jo: Lelandus.

'On this watery land, which nature and art have contributed to keep damp, are scattered palaces and hovels… The wretched dwellings of the poor are scattered haphazard around [the factories]… Heaps of dung, rubble from buildings, putrid, stagnant pools are found here and there amongst the houses… Amid this noisome labyrinth from time to time one is astonished at the sight of fine stone buildings with Corinthian columns… From this foul drain the greatest stream of human industry flows out to fertilise the whole world. From this filthy sewer pure gold flows. Here humanity attains its most complete development and its most brutish; here civilisation works its miracles, and civilised man is turned back into a savage.'

Count Alexis de Tocqueville, 1840

'Certainly Manchester is the most wonderful city of modern times.'

Benjamin Disraeli, *Coningsby*, 1844

But the most horrible spot… lies… immediately south west of Oxford Road and is known as Little Ireland. The race that lives in these ruinous cottages, behind broken windows, mended with oilskin, sprung doors, and rotten door-posts, or in dark, wet cellars, in measureless filth and stench… must surely have reached the lowest stage of humanity.

Frederick Engels, *The Condition of the Working Class in England*, 1847

'[The] Brothers Cowper removed the manufacture of their printing machines from London, to Manchester. There they found skilled and energetic workmen, ready to carry their plans into effect… I compared them with the workmen I had seen in London, and found them superior. They were men of greater energy of character; their minds were more capacious; their ingenuity was more inventive.'

James Nasmyth, engineer, *Autobiography*, 1885

'Far, far away in the distance, on that flat plain, you might see the motionless cloud of smoke hanging over a great town, and that was Manchester – ugly, smoky Manchester; dear busy, earnest, noble-working Manchester; where their children had been born, and where, perhaps, some lay buried; where their homes were, and where God had cast their lives, and told them to work out their destiny.'

Elizabeth Gaskell, *Libbie Marsh's Three Eras*, 1847

'"Eh, lad," quoth Simon, rubbing down his knees as he sat, "aw've manny a time bin i' just sich a 'strait atween two; 'but aw allus steered moi coorse by yon big book, and tha' mun do t' seame. Thah munnot think what thah loikes, or what thah dunnot loike; but thah mun do reet, chuse what comes or goes. It is na reet to steeal; and to look on an' consent to a thief is to be a thief. Thi first duty's to thi God, an' thi next to thi payrents (if tha' had anny), an' thi next to thi measter. Thah's gi'en the chap fair warnin', an' if he wunnot tak it th' faut's noan thoine."'

Mrs G. Linnaeus Banks, *The Manchester Man*, 1874

'For Manchester is the place where people do things... "Don't talk about what you are going to do, do it." That is the Manchester habit. And in the past through the manifestation of this quality the word Manchester became a synonym for energy and freedom and the right to do and to think without shackles.'

From *What the Judge Saw* by Judge Parry, 1912

'(Mancunians) make an affectation of candour and trade a little on their county's reputation for uncouthness.'

From *Hobson's Choice* by Harold Brighouse of Eccles, 1917

'Manchester... the belly and guts of the Nation.'

***The Road to Wigan Pier*, 1937, by George Orwell**

Contemporary Comments

'When I was young I did not see the beauty of the Manchester streets. I used to go into the country painting landscapes and the like. Then one day I saw it... suddenly I saw the beauty of the streets and the crowds.'

L.S. Lowry, 1972

'Manchester has everything but good looks... the only place in England which escapes our characteristic vice of snobbery.'

Historian A.J.P. Taylor

'In those days [pre-Second World War] for a Mancunian to visit [London] was an exercise in condescension. London was a day behind Manchester in the arts, in commercial cunning, in economic philosophy... Manchester was generous and London was not.'

Anthony Burgess, Manc novelist, *Little Wilson and Big God*, 1986

'Manchester's got everything except a beach.'

Ian Brown, The Stone Roses

'Sarcasm is a Manchester trait.'

Peter Hook of Joy Division

'When Blur first started and we were playing Manchester, the Haçienda was the place to go. That was where a lot of exciting stuff was happening and London was pretty dead.'

Graham Coxon of Blur

'The first time I came here I knew it was a place rich in culture... Manchester reminds me very much of San Francisco. Even the weather's the same... When I go back home to California, people ask me if I'm homesick. How can you be homesick in Manchester? There's so much going on here.'

Mark Delaney Robinson, captain of Manchester Giants, 1997

'Anthony Wilson says that for a big City, Manchester is just small enough. It's true. People know each other, collaborate, cross-pollinate. Ideas can mix and match. It's easy to get things moving. But Manchester's size also makes the social processes more visible... You can see how things are developing. Where they might end up is another matter... Will everything keep spinning and never actually fall down? Who knows. But Manchester, as Mancs love to tell you, has been ahead of the game. Perhaps it'll be the first place to show us whether our new cities work.'

From 'Manchester Divided' by Jim McClellan,
***Esquire Magazine*, June 1997**

'Lost in Manchester's city centre – architectural chronicler Nicolas Pevsner called it "one of the most confusing city centres in England" – one senses Manchester's enduring grittiness, particularly in the bohemian Northern Quarter. But much of it has followed American cities' example of transforming industrial zones into "warehouse districts". Manchester's cotton mills, insurance halls and warehouses have become lofts, restaurants, bars and graphic design HQs.'

From 'A bright outlook in the North' by Oliver Bennett,
***Daily Express*, October 1998**

'The thing about Manchester is... it all comes from here.'
Noel Gallagher, pointing to his heart, BBC2, September 1998

'Behold the ingenuities of civic pride: ugly we may be, but our ugly's bigger than yours.'

Howard Jacobson, Jewish Mancunian and novelist,
***The Independent*, December 1999**

'Manchester... the embodiment of a great city.'
Norman Foster (Baron Foster of Thames Bank),
Mancunian architect

Famous For...

Cotton mills

Manchester Capitalism and the Free Trade movement

Madchester, Oasis, Simply Red, the Halle Orchestra, the BeeGees, Russell Watson...

Comedians

Derby matches with real emotion

Splitting the atom

Coronation Street

The Cooperative Wholesale Society

Ben Brierley, Victorian dialect poet

Backdrops for the films *Sherlock Holmes*, *Captain America*, *Alfie*, *51st State*

Infamous For...

Gunchester

Scallies – the Northern 'Chav'

Terry Christian

Shameless

Roof-slate chucking riots at HM Prison Strangeways

Moss Side

The lethal alcoholic concoctions of the Blob Shop

Strangeways Prison

Opium-eater Thomas de Quincy

B of the Bang sculpture – good on paper, but a disaster in reality

Nineteenth-century slums

Dark Satanic Mills

Manchester Then & Now

Letters to the Press

'Is it not time Manchester City Council stood up for one of its proud and distinguished areas? The city-slicker advertising brigade, of which many are in the Town Hall, are intent on killing off the area of Bradford and replacing it with a more fashionable and media-friendly name of Eastlands. I see from letters in your Postbag, the ex-pats of Bradford, of which I am one, are not willing to allow this to happen. Bradford was once a major industrial area of Manchester, with Bradford Colliery and Bradford Gas Works among the many engineering companies in the district. The area died for a few years due to housing clearance but, like the phoenix, it is rising from the ashes. SportCity, which incorporates the City of Manchester Stadium, a new modern constabulary complex and possibly the largest Asda store in the city, are just some of the new additions. The councillor for Bradford should stand up for his ward. I notice there is a large official road sign on the A34 saying "Welcome to Burnage". Maybe such a sign could maintain the identity of an area that refuses to disappear?'

Brian Howard, south Manchester, 17 December 2010

'Regarding Jeremy Clarkson's comments on the re-location of *Top Gear* to Salford – how dare he slate Salford? He forgets I, like many other people, pay his salary through the licence fee. I'm astounded that he gets a reported £2m a year. How can the BBC justify this amount for an outspoken, loudmouth snob who only likes to put down anyone or anything that he doesn't like just because he has a good bank balance and he is fortunate to live in a lovely part of the country. Salford may not offer thatched cottages and surrounding pretty villages, but what it does have is very genuine down-to-earth friendly folk who would go that extra mile to help anyone in need. I myself was born down south in Surrey, but we moved up north 60 years ago and are still here – that speaks volumes. If Jeremy Clarkson or anyone else at the BBC in London are still whingeing about moving to MediaCity in Salford, then let them stay there. There are plenty of people here in Salford willing to take up their jobs.'

Infuriated reader, Stretford, Thursday 14 July 2011

Rebellious Manchester

'Peterloo' remains the single most striking incident in Manchester's long history of discontent and protest. In Saint Peter's Fields, now the site of St Peter's Square, a vast crowd assembled in August 1819. Their slogans included the Radical demand for an extension of voting rights, as well as issues of more immediate concern to the millworkers, such as an end to gentry-favouring protectionist laws that kept the price of staple foodstuffs artificially high.

Men, women and children had come from all the surrounding towns to protest and hear the speeches of 'Orator' Hunt. To the Reactionary civic authorities, however, the memory of heads rolling in Paris boulevards was too fresh for them to tolerate such unsanctioned displays of proletarian strength, and the Cheshire Yeomanry were called in to disperse the gathering. Sabres were drawn and lives lost. Fatalities numbered two dozen, but many more were grievously wounded. In mockery of the 'courage' of the cavalrymen, the outrage was christened 'Peterloo', in contrast to the recent Battle of Waterloo.

'In all hearts that witnessed Peterloo, stands written, as in fire-characters... a legible balance-account of grim vengeance... payable readily at sight with compound interest! Such things should be avoided as the very pestilence.'

Thomas Carlyle, historian, 1843

Buildings & Architecture

The mills are now either gone or converted into flats, as Manchester embarks upon a new, post-industrial phase in its long and varied life, and new building projects demonstrate that there's life in the old dog yet. Thankfully, much remains of each previous incarnation, and it is now quite possible to find views that include Roman ramparts, eighteenth-century canals, Victorian mills and twenty-first century ultra-modern luxury high-rises.

The confines of space have ensured that almost any vista in the modern city will be definitively Mancunian – a juxtaposition of styles. When planning has been at its best, the new serves to accentuate the old, releasing individual historic features from the accumulated dingy clutter of the post-war years, allowing stone mouldings and glazed tiles to be reflected in the light mirror walls of the new structures.

Most characteristic of all is the ubiquitous High Victorian mixture of red brick and buff sandstone. Industrial Manchester, now chiefly represented by converted warehouses and mills, itself shows variation in style, from puritan boxes of brick and slate to mock-Venetian palazzio façades.

Victorian civic pride left its grand mark on our city with Alfred Waterhouse's 1877 Town Hall, a masterpiece of neo-Gothic, decorated inside and out with monuments and murals to Manchester worthies of all periods.

Watts Warehouse, 1856, now the Britannia Hotel, is the best example of the extravagances of the early industrial magnates of the city. Extremely eclectic, each storey has its own style – Egyptian, Italian Renaissance, Elizabethan, French Renaissance, Flemish and Gothic.

Ornate gave way in time to bold, and if the head is lifted to scan the rooftops of Manchester, a collection of Art Deco to rival Miami is revealed, with Sunlight House as its best example.

Wartime bombing destroyed much, and the rebuilding left many ugly oblongs on our skyline. Despite its post-IRA bomb makeover, the Brutalist 1970s Arndale Centre – a vast shopping mall – remains the most cited architectural blight in the city. Estimates from 1968 of an £11.5 million total cost proved seriously out, the final total coming to the £100 million mark. The tower has attracted plenty of harsh descriptions down the years, from 'bile yellow' to 'vomit', with numerous references to 'toilets' and 'public lavatories'.

Manchester is aiming high. Stylish new sky-scrapers are popping up all the time, and natives returning after time away are left quite disorientated. Back in 1962, our CIS Tower was briefly the UK's tallest building at 387ft (118 metres). Architect Ian Simpson has left his mark at both ends of Deansgate, in the Beetham Tower and No. 1 Deansgate. The Beetham Tower was finished in 2006 and reaches forty-seven storeys, 168 metres or 551ft – the tallest outside London – and is notable for its slight overhang halfway up, containing a sky-bar with glass floor panels for the brave to stand on.

Desirable and expensive residential properties both find their superlatives here, attracting highly paid Premier League footballers. The year 2010 saw Gary Neville's three-storey flat in the Beetham Tower put on the market at £4 million. Its architect's flat, further up the tower, has almost thrice the space however – 12,500 sq ft of it – and is valued at twice the price. No. 1 Deansgate, rather distressingly perched on several diagonally placed steel tubes, has also appealed to this market (its penthouses breaking local records by selling at £1.5 million in 2002), and is the tallest all-steel residential building in the UK.

But records are soon broken in the new Manchester; another mixed leisure/residential fifty-eight-storey skyscraper with a height of 188 metres (617ft) is under construction, the Picadilly Tower. On a smaller scale, the nine-floor flat in the tower of the converted Saint George's church in Hulme is the tallest single apartment in the UK.

Museums

Manchester Museum contains Egyptian mummies, stuffed animals of every stripe and living poison-arrow frogs – all rub shoulders here on Oxford Road, alongside Roman altars commissioned by the first known Mancunians.

The Museum of Science and Industry ('MOSI') is housed on the territory of the world's first passenger railway station.

Pump House People's History Museum commemorates the struggle of working men and women for dignity and control over their fate.

Manchester Art Gallery and the **Whitworth Art Gallery** – Pre-Raphaelites abound!

The Imperial War Museum North is found at Salford Quays – a former Luftwaffe target.

The **Lowry Centre** celebrates the life and work of L.S. Lowry, artistic chronicler of industrial Manchester.

Manchester Jewish Museum is an old Sephardic synagogue.

Manchester Transport Museum looks after many an old tram, bus and carriage.

Greater Manchester Fire Service Museum honours our brave fire-fighters.

The year 2012 brings the opening of the **National Football Museum** in Cathedral Square.

Parks

The official metropolitan district of Manchester's largest park, and its highest point, is the award-winning Heaton Park. With the neoclassical Heaton Hall as its focal point, it encompasses over 640 acres of open lawns, a boating lake, golf course, ornamental gardens, an ever-popular petting zoo, and has superb views of the city and surrounding hills from the hilltop observatory. The Earl of Wilton sold the park to the city in 1902.

Closer to the city centre, we have the old Victorian parks, set up for the 'leisure and health of the people': Phillips Park, Queen's Park, Clayton Vale and Brookdale Park.

Open Spaces

In the city centre, these chiefly consist of demolished church sites like St John's Gardens in Castlefield and All Saints' Park by the university. Most interesting of all is perhaps Angel Meadow. Until recently, a large part of this former churchyard (St Michael's was demolished in 1935) was covered in large stone flags, making a playground of the site of a mass grave. Now a pleasantly landscaped area of grass and trees, this was once the burial ground for one of the most notorious slums of the city.

New open spaces have been created with new development, notably by the Urbis in Cathedral Square, and the 'Green Quarter' where a formerly undesirable damp dip has been colonised by chic new apartment blocks.

Local Fauna & Flora

As a railway and canal node, Manchester is rich in fireweed, otherwise known as Rosebay Willowherb or *Epilobium angustifolium*. Brownland sites and railway verges have spread this weed far and wide, making it a characteristic feature of the great Mancunian 'croft' ecosystem. The croft constitutes an area of temporarily waste ground, typically found after the demolition of a Victorian mill. The soil base is chiefly red brick rubble, with some variety added in terms of dead cats, dumped mattresses, rusty nails and other tetanus-bearing sharp-edged objects.

Another successful plant that has made crumbling brickwalls and blocked drainpipes its inner city home is the *Buddleia davidii*. The slightest indentation in a wall is enough for the seeds of this not unattractive flowering shrub to find a footing, providing a magnet for butterflies and bumblebees.

Beyond rats and other scurrying creatures of the dingier nooks and crannies, animal life consists mostly of birds. Pigeons do well enough, delighting onlookers with their courtship dances and fascinatingly mangled feet. The elaborate network of waterways is home to a fleet of hardy Mallard ducks and Canada geese, especially around Castlefield. Magpies are perhaps the most striking avine residents, however, and cackle knowingly at pedestrians.

Home-Grown Businesses

'These Mambari are very enterprising merchants...
They bring Manchester goods into the heart of Africa;
these cotton prints look so wonderful that the Makololo
could not believe them to be the work of mortal
hands... An attempt at explanation of our manufactures
usually elicits the expression, "Truly ye are gods!"'
David Livingstone's memoirs of 1850s-60s inner Africa

Cottonopolis was an alias of the young Manchester, but
there's plenty of energy left from those smoky days and
Manchester today presents one of the better cases of
'getting on with life' in the Post-Industrial Age. For a while
in the 1960s and '70s it did seem hard to creep out from
under the shadow of the hulking derelict factories, but
most of these that have survived are now shiny downtown
apartments, studios and offices, so we must be doing
something right!

But that's not to say that all the older generation firms have
gone. Some of the best known have grown with the city
itself: **Vimto** has been a much loved Manc brand since 1912,
when its inventor Noel Nichols shortened the name of this
mysterious fruity drink from the unwieldy 'Vim-Tonic'.

Thirsty Mancunians after something more alcoholic have
been downing pints of local ale **J.W. Lees** since 1828 – look
out for their *Coronation Street* Ale. **Joseph Holts** started
up in 1860, since which they have expanded to their
present 127 pubs in the Greater Manchester area. **Hydes
Brewery** appeared soon after in 1863, and is now open for
visits to connoisseurs in the evenings. Their older sibling,
Boddingtons, sadly ran dry in 2005, after a brewing history
of 227 years, and the old landmark of its lettered smokestack
was toppled soon after. RIP.

E. HADER pinxit. 1881. Gesetzlich geschützt.

Phot. u. Verl. v. Sophus Williams, Berlin W.

Largest Employers

The Corn Exchange has long since closed, but cereal giant **Kellogg's** plant at Trafford Park is the largest manufacturing employer here today. 1,000 people work here on the vast 130,000 square foot site to provide Mancs with their breakfast cornflakes.

Mancunian engineering heritage lives on with **Mono Group** in Audenshaw, where 'progressing cavity pumps, grinders, screens and oilfield products' are produced. Chemical and metallurgical research and development are also pursued at their laboratories.

Renold plc owes its name to the Swiss Hans Renold who purchased a small chain-making business in Salford in 1879, and production continues of this vital component in most machines, including almost all forms of transport.

Though the Cooperative movement was started up by the Rochdale Pioneers, the **Cooperative Wholesale Society** has its national headquarters in our city centre, with the prominent CIS tower. As this book goes to print, work is well underway for yet another iconic landmark connected with the CWS, the NOMA development, underlining its continuing relationship with our city.

Political Figures

Wartime Prime Minister **Sir David Lloyd George** was born here in 1863, but there are plenty of other politicians with a deeper connection to the place than the 'Welsh Wizard', who left while still a baby.

Richard Cobden is probably the most influential to date. Born in 1804, he fought for free trade – a still popular ideal, though slightly less to our advantage now that our city isn't producing the lion's share of world manufacturing! For his efforts to repeal the infamous Corn Laws which kept the poorest of society near starvation levels, Cobden received his statue in St Ann's Square.

Moss Side's **Emmeline Pankhurst** (1858-1928) needs less of an introduction, as her militant campaigning for 'Votes for Women' captured the imagination of the public, even though it has overshadowed the arguably more effective work of the less disruptive contemporary suffragists.

Labour politician **Harold Lever**'s (1914-1995) Mancunian credentials couldn't be stronger: he was born here and attended both our grammar school and university, and later acted as MP from the 1940s to the 1970s. Made Baron Lever of Manchester in 1979, he fought in old age for the cancelling of Third World debt.

Scientific Discoveries

Even before the founding of UMIST (University of Manchester Institute of Science and Technology) in its 1825 incarnation of the Mechanics' Institute, Manchester was home to a level of scientific activity befitting its position at the forefront of practical technological application. Our Literary and Philosophical Society, one of the oldest in the country (1781), has long contributed to profitable cross-pollination of ideas between our local thinkers.

Of all the great names, **James Prescott Joule** (1818-1889) is probably most familiar to those less scientifically minded, even if the kilo-Joule is more familiar than the man himself. To him we owe much of the modern practical and theoretical knowledge of energy.

John Dalton belonged to an earlier generation (1766-1844) for whom practical experiment was still a novel accompaniment to philosophical inquiry. Though his Town Hall mural shows him engaged in the hands-on task of sucking 'marsh gas' from a swamp, Dalton is chiefly remembered for his early demonstrations of atomic theory.

For actual proof of Dalton's theory, we are indebted to **Ernest Rutherford** (1871–1937), whose Manchester work with radiation 'photographed' the 'shadow' of the long-sought atom with nucleus, electrons and all.

Nobel prizes keep on coming to Manchester University, most notable lately for Russian-born **Professors Andrei Geim** and **Kostya Novoselov's** discovery of graphene – a previously unknown form of carbon that promises to be of immense value in nanotechnology.

Local Characters, Past & Present

Though **Frank Sidebottom's** home town of Timperley is found on the wrong side of the Mersey, the papier-maché-headed crooner's Manchester ties are unquestionable. Net surfers are encouraged to seek out his 'Manchester Medley' in which he paid homage – in his own inimitable style – to the city's musical heritage.

The eternally-tanned antiques expert and television personality **David Dickinson** is another local treasure, best known for his show *Bargain Hunt*. His down-to-earth catchphrases – such as 'cheap as chips' – and ready charm certainly mark out his Manchester origins. His appearance on the genealogical programme *Who Do You Think You Are?* also gave a fascinating glimpse into our oft-overlooked Armenian community.

If Boltonians will forgive his inclusion, **Fred Dibnah** should be remembered for promoting Mancunian industrial heritage. Ironically, as a steeplejack he was also responsible for flattening a good part of it. Some 1970s TV appearances first introduced viewers to Fred's utterances of 'Bluddy Ell!' and 'Did yer like that?', and he later turned presenter himself, losing none of his trademark manner of speech.

Mary Ann Lee was born on Toad Lane in 1736. Convinced that total chastity was vital to salvation, she fled our worldly city to found the United Society of Believers in Christ's Second Appearing, AKA 'the Shakers', in New York. Though the sect's taste in furniture is their chief legacy, Mary Ann deserves to be remembered as a peculiarly outspoken and forceful woman for her time.

Mark Addy (1838-1890) was a Salford hero who saved well over fifty people from drowning in the Irwell. This feat grows in heroism when the state of the river at the time is borne in mind (earning it the nickname 'the Sewage Canal'). His final rescue, that of a small boy, led to his death at fifty-two. He is remembered in the name of a footbridge and a modern riverside pub on the Irwell.

Crimes, Court Cases & Mysteries

Gunchester – This nickname was earned in the 1990s for the drug-related violence that then reached its peak in the Moss Side, Longsight and Hulme districts, associated with the clashes between rival West-Indian derived gangs. The year 2004 even saw gang members running through hospital wards with guns drawn after one shootout had hospitalised their associates. A series of police operations and multi-agency initiatives have resulted in thirty-year sentences for the ringleaders, and there is hope that new community-wide strategies will continue to prevent future gun murders in the city.

During the Second World War, **Herbert Winstanley** turned his Rusholme end-terrace into a forger's headquarters: not of ration books, German documents or military papers, but simply of £5 notes to satisfy his gambling habit. After several years counterfeiting, which had convinced the police of the existence of an organised gang, the 'King of Forgers' let his guard slip and was caught handing over two notes with the same serial number at the dog track. Dozens of notes were found stacked in bundles at his home and drying on washing lines over his bed.

Populous cities will have their underworlds, but let us just leave the matter with a remark on how, when the **Kray twins** sought to extend their business affairs to our Northern Capital, they were received on the platform at Piccadilly Station by a welcome committee of local 'civic-minded private gentlemen' who, after a brief discussion, promptly ensured that the brothers were placed back onto a train for London...

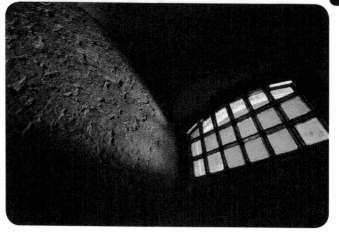

Manchester folk's ambivalent attitude to this sphere of life is commemorated in popular verse:

Collyhurst Road

When I was young and lazy, as lazy as can be,
I said goodbye to the mother-in-law and I went off to sea.
We sailed with Captain Skipper on the good ship
Mary Anne
And we all set sail down Collyhurst Road in a Black
Mariah van.

Chorus:

Collyhurst Road, I am forsaken,
And it's not that my poor heart is aching.
It's the whisky and the beer that I've been taking
For that charming little girl down Collyhurst Road.

Well, the Law got hold of me and they put me in
Number Three.
They said 'You are a Collyhurst lad and you'll never get
away from me.
And next time you go sailing, it won't be the *Mary Anne*;
It'll be down Collyhurst Road to the Collyhurst Nick in
a Black Mariah van.'

Repeat Chorus

Ghosts & the Unexplained

Timber-framed **Ordsall Hall** is our most haunted building. Remembering the days when the hall was more rundown, older local residents mention the 'spirit children' they'd played with in the then much wilder grounds. Several members of the old Radclyffe gentry family haunt their former home, the 'White Lady' being a certain heartbroken Margaret of that name. 'Alexander' is even reputed to have retained his mortal interest in pinching ladies' bottoms, while the dark, silent and staring 'John' is said to have a far less benevolent presence.

The former cholera pits of **Angel Meadow** have seen their fair share of mysterious apparitions, taking their name from angels seen hovering over the site, grieving for the poor victims of these epidemics. Sightings are said to occur mainly at the Angel Steps leading down from the present park...

Manchester Under Attack

'Dalton's records, carefully preserved for a century, were destroyed during the World War II bombing of Manchester. It is not only the living who are killed in war.'
Sci-fi author Isaac Asimov

Manchester, a major seaport and centre of munitions and weapon production, was a perfect Luftwaffe target, and experienced its share of the Blitz. An early Christmas present from Hitler, the nights of the 22 and 23 December 1940 saw a major bombardment, in which over 1,000 lives were lost and many more wounded, thanks to 500 tonnes of explosives and almost 2,000 incendiary bombs. Much of the uglier post-war architecture can be forgiven for the need to patch up the destruction wrought on the city then.

Another less-expected attack took place in recent times, giving Mancs another chance to show their characteristic resilience to the world. No sooner had the smoke cleared after the 15 June 1996 IRA bomb on Corporation Street than plans were put into action with a collective civic determination to turn even this near miss (that nobody had died in such a bustling shopping quarter was little short of a miracle) into a victory of the indomitable and ever-practical Manc spirit. Indeed, the most common response you'll evoke from locals on the attack will typically be, 'Thi've dun us a favour!' The city seized the opportunity to redevelop the retail district and actually move two of our oldest buildings (the pre-industrial Shambles formed by the Wellington Inn and Sinclair's Oyster bar) into a new, better positioned site by the cathedral.

Local Lingo

Foreigners armed with phrases like 'How do you do?' are little prepared for Manchester, where the traditional greeting of 'Are you alright?' is mostly whittled down to a disyllabic 'Y'awrigh'?' or even 'Y'awree'?'

'Excuse me' is rather 'Eeyar, Mate/Luv' (i.e. likewise shortened from a more intelligible 'Here you are') – used also when passing someone an object. Certain stock phrases have become almost indivisible parts of speech in themselves, such as 'Jerwannabrew?' and 'Do-uzabrew'. 'Oh-aye-you-n'all' is a very Manc introductory phrase designed to stun and disarm an opponent before delivering the knockout blow, usually on the lines of 'what've yer dun wi my [insert object]?'

The pronoun 'I' is often 'A', the vowel 'U' always rhymes with 'bull', and 'A' has a distinctly open quality. 'T' between vowels is frequently 'K', as in 'bockle o' beer', 'ospickal', 'Scockland', and 'you lickle bleeder'.

Past participles of verbs are routinely abandoned as unnecessary. I was in my twenties when I finally figured out the peculiar nature and purpose of 'written' as opposed to 'wrote'.

Most common local terms:

Nowt, **owt**, and **summat** – 'Nothing', 'anything' and 'something' ('everything' somehow escaped similar treatment).

Myther – Perhaps the most characteristic of all, roughly translated 'bother' or 'annoyance', a noun and a verb: 'What was he mythering about?' 'A can't be mythered.' 'You mythering lickle get!' 'A'm sorry to myther you, but...'

Hanging – Adjective, 'disgusting', 'repulsive', 'horrible'.

Sken-eyed – 'Cross-eyed'.

Cob – A roundish loaf, or 'to throw', both from 'cobblestone'.

Brew – Local pronunciation of 'brow' in the sense of 'small hill', especially over a canal bridge.

Bob, Bobbins – 'Rubbish' or 'nonsense', a term from our cotton spinning heritage, often figuring as a euphemism for another disyllabic word beginning 'bo-'...

For expletives, the standard Anglo-Saxon ejaculations are employed, but in the contracted forms 'Dy Ell! and 'Kin ell!, but the term 'cock' should not be taken as offensive; along with 'Luv' and 'Ar Kid', it is a typical endearment, most often used for close relatives, to the horror of any dirty-minded Sutherners who happen to be in earshot.

Least & Most Favourite Scenes

Festivals

We boast a year-round cultural life to suit our position as England's Northern Capital. Annual highlights include:

Manchester Comedy Festival

Manchester Jazz Festival

Manchester Literature Festival

Manchester Pride

Manchester Day

Food and Drink Festival

Science Festival (biggest in the UK)

Feel Good Festival

Famous People Today

Norman Foster, Baron Foster of Thames Bank (1935-), grew up in Levenshulme, attending Burnage Grammar, and came to dominate the world architecture of a generation. He is responsible for the London Gherkin, the Millau Viaduct in France (tallest in the world), Berlin's noted Reichstag restoration, Hong Kong's HSBC main building, and the new Wembley Stadium, among many other projects, some of which are yet to be completed.

John Thaw (1942-2002), TV's Inspector Morse, grew up in Burnage, working as a Manchester fruit-market porter before adding more than thirty years of acting to his name, earning a BAFTA and a CBE. His famous 'Shut it!' catchphrase made *The Sweeney*, and his popularity in his most famous role may be judged from the viewing stats for his final three episodes as Morse: over 18 million.

Ricky 'the Hitman' Hatton (1978-) represented boxing Manchester on a world level from 1997 to 2009. The 'Pride of Hyde' is a great MCFC fan, entering the ring to the tune 'Blue Moon'.

Few Mancunians watching *The Pink Panther* films realised that Inspector Clouseau's oriental man-servant Cato was Manchester-born **Bert Kwouk** (1930-). Later appearing in *Last of the Summer Wine*, he received his OBE in 2011.

TV's Lovejoy, actor **Ian McShane** (1942-) grew up in Urmston, and regularly appears in Hollywood blockbusters like *Pirates of the Caribbean*, while still finding time to provide narration for the latest wildlife documentaries.

Historian **Michael Wood** (1948-) grew up in Moston and Wythenshawe and carved out a role in TV documentaries, leading viewers to exotic locations in the *Footsteps of Alexander the Great*, and deep into English history in *Domesday*.

The most famous living Failsworth man, **Michael Atherton OBE** (1968-) captained the England Cricket side for a record fifty-four Test Matches.

Musical Manchester

Giving birth to the modern world, it's no surprise that Manchester has consistently led the way in modern popular music.

Local milkman Freddie Garrity gathered a group in the early 1960s to form **Freddie and the Dreamers**, releasing a steady stream of songs including 'I'm Telling You Now'. Another Manchester group of the early 1960s with US success in the 'British Invasion' years was **Herman's Hermits** with hits such as 'I'm Into Something Good'. Spanning the 1960s and '70s, and still going, **The Hollies** are probably best known now for their 'He Ain't Heavy, He's My Brother'.

Manchester will not be denied a place in folk history either. Salford-born **Ewan McColl** (1915-1989) gave our city its most famous song, despite its adoption by the Irish! 'Dirty Old Town' immortalised the still intact factory-scapes of its day in 1949, and has been recorded by many folk singers since. McColl coupled music with politics, but his other work has thankfully outlived his 'Ballad of Stalin'...

Barry, Robin and Maurice Gibb were born Manx, but grew up Mancs in Chorlton. Their unique harmonies as the **BeeGees** remain instantly recognisable, and the trio wrote songs for many other performers too. Performing continuously from the late 1950s, even the 2003 death of Maurice has not deterred his brothers from carrying on into a fifth decade of music-making.

In the 1980s, Manchester found its most distinctive voice with the development of the **Madchester** scene, and Tony Wilson's Haçienda nightclub.

It started off in 1976 with **Joy Division**. Then **Morrisey** and **Johnny Mar**'s songwriting partnership gave us **The Smiths**, and 'There Is a Light That Never Goes Out'. **New Order**'s 1980s 'Post-Punk' electronics were another great success, their 'Blue Monday' being the highest-selling 12in single ever.

The name of an Oldham carpet-shop united forever with music history as the **Inspiral Carpets** formed in 1983. Madchester then produced **Happy Mondays** (1980), and **The Stone Roses** (1983) who promise to release a new album for 2011. Inspired by the Haçienda years, the **Chemical Brothers** made Manchester a centre of electronic music back in 1991.

The early 1990s were the classical years of Mick Hucknall's **Simply Red**, bringing songs like 'Holding Back The Years' and the famous cover of 'Money's Too Tight (To Mention)'.

From the first letter of their name **M People** identified themselves very closely with our city and enjoyed success throughout the 1990s. Notable tracks include 'How Can I Love You More?' and the upbeat 'Search For The Hero Inside Yourself'.

Probably the biggest contemporary Manchester band, **Oasis** took their name from an Inspiral Carpets poster on the Gallagher brothers' bedroom wall. Known as much for the stormy relations between Liam and Noel and their occasionally outspoken comments, this group managed to influence a host of younger musicians from their beginnings in 1991 to the ultimate break-up in 2009.

More recent bands that may stand the test of time include **Badly Drawn Boy**, **Jim Noir**, **Doves**, **Elbow**, **I Am Kloot**, **The Ting Tings**, **Delphic** and **Hurts**.

Funny Manchester

Les Dawson was born in Collyhurst in 1931. He passed away in 1993 after a career spanning the golden age of the clubs and television. His astonishingly pliable facial features are sadly missed.

For Ancoats born **Bernard Manning** (1930-2007), his Russian Jewish and Irish roots were ever his get-out clause for some pretty risqué ethnic humour, but he never let the tender sensibilities of others hold him back in the pursuit of a laugh at his World Famous Embassy Club (sic).

Mrs Merton, or rather **Caroline Aherne** (1963-) hails from Wythenshawe, and began her comic career alongside Frank Sidebottom, ending up with her own chatshow, where she delivered the immortal line, 'So, what first attracted you to the millionaire Paul Daniels?'

Steve Coogan, born 1965 in the suburb of Middleton, heads the latest generation of Manc comics, and is best known for his satirical characters of which daytime TV presenter Alan Partridge is best known, but it is the duo of Paul and Pauline Calf that draw most on his local background.

Peter Kay (Bolton, 1973-) has also crossed the divide between traditional stand up and televised comedy. His *Phoenix Nights* sitcom celebrated the clubland roots of the North-Western comedy phenomenon, spawning the spin-off Max and Paddy act with his co-star and fellow comic **Paddy McGuinness** (Farnworth, 1973-). Kay made headlines recently with his box-office records: all 200,000 tickets for his 2010 Manchester tour sold out in under an hour, and he continues to fill our MEN Arena night after night.

Sports

The mills brought vast armies of workers to Manchester, thousands of hardworking men in need of entertainment on their days off. This demand was met in part by football, a sport which has kept the name Manchester on the lips of the world despite King Cotton's fall.

But there is more than football! Old Trafford itself is home to **Lancashire's County Cricket Club**, and the MEN Arena's ability to double as an ice rink allowed Manchester to watch a rather rougher sport than the dainty Premiership football, thanks to our ice-hockey champions **Manchester Storm**. From being the most supported such team in British history, it sadly disbanded in 2002, though its legacy is carried on by Altrincham's **Manchester Phoenix**. Basketball's **Manchester Giants** experienced similar cash problems, dissolving in 2001.

Another page was turned in our sporting history with the hosting of the 2002 **Commonwealth Games** in a new modern stadium, now home to MCFC. The Sport City complex that grew up in this former brownlands site has, in the intervening decade, never ceased to build on this success: the striking Velodrome, athletics and squash facilities living up to their 'From Grassroots to Greatness' slogan. Special mention is deserved for the **British Paralympics** team who train here, an almost certain bet in international competitions such as the Paralympic World Cup, held in our city for the seventh time in 2011.

Needless to say, Manchester has a keen eye on the coming 2012 London Olympiad!

Teams

From the depths of the Amazon to Outer Mongolia, any Mancunian can expect to hear the phrase 'Manchester United!' as soon as he reveals his origins. In the city itself, however, their rivals Manchester City have always claimed what must be one of the most impressively loyal fan bases in the long history of football. As if to reward this, recent years have seen something of a turnaround in fortunes, with Gulf oil money making the Blues the richest club in football.

Manchester United
Home colours: red

Founded in 1878 as Newton Heath LYR (Lancashire and Yorkshire Railway) FC

Renamed in 1902 as Manchester United FC

Home ground: Old Trafford

Capacity: 75,957

Owners: the Glazer family, USA

Manager: Sir Alex Ferguson

Manchester City
Home colours: blue

Founded in 1880 as St Mark's (West Gorton) FC

Renamed in 1887 as Ardwick Association FC

Renamed in 1894 as Manchester City FC

Home Ground: Formerly Maine Road, and now City of Manchester Stadium at Sport City

Capacity: 47,805

Owner: Sheikh Mansour bin Zayed Al Nahyan, Abu Dhabi

Manager: Roberto Mancini

Secret Manchester

One of our best-kept secrets is **Chetham's Library** in the grounds of Chetham's School of Music. The oldest free public library in the Anglosphere, it grew from a bequest of Humphrey Chetham, a local merchant anxious that his fortune benefit his home town after his death. Built around a mediaeval monastic cloister and former Great Hall of our Norman barons, it comprises some of our oldest architecture, with rich red masonry in the local sandstone.

Other secret treasures owe their existence to the city's Roman Catholic minority. The 'Hidden Gem', **Saint Mary's church** on Mulberry Street, dates from 1794, a time when discretion on the part of non-established confessions was still felt sensible. Its position and exterior are little preparation for the riches within. **Gorton Monastery** shows no such timidity, standing out in its surroundings more now than it had done even at its 1872 opening.

The preservation of mediaeval wooden architecture in such a metropolis as Greater Manchester may surprise, but old manorial halls still stand in the midst of industrial units and modern housing projects. See **Ordsall Hall** (in our 'ghosts' section!), and Humphrey Chetham's **Clayton Hall**. Further afield, **Hall i'th'Wood** is an even more picturesque anachronism in unapologetically industrial Bolton, home to Samuel Crompton – 1779 inventor of the Spinning Mule.

Manchester Women

A glance through the older history of our town reveals that a high proportion of civil unrest has been sparked by *Mancunienne* brawlers in the old Market Stead Lane. Riled at occasionally exorbitant prices, these Amazons favoured direct action over the niceties of diplomacy and would seize sacks of potatoes and wheat, spilling the contents over the ground for their comrades. Such escapades frequently ended in riots and full-blown troop mobilisations, as happened in 1757.

Manchester's peculiar brand of femininity became an export commodity in 1912, in the form of radical Suffragette activism: Mary Leigh flung an axe at the carriage of the Mayor of Dublin, set fire to a theatre's curtains and threw a burning chair into the orchestra pit. Her career in the movement involved several cases of stoning Prime Ministers' carriages and axe-related rooftop vandalism incidents, nine arrests and more than fifteen months in prison, during which she underwent force-feeding.

The tradition of such strong no-nonsense womanhood carries on, entering popular culture through such portrayals as those of Corrie's Ena Sharples or Bet Lynch, Les Dawson and Roy Barraclough's Cissie and Ada, and most recently in Steve Coogan's Pauline Calf.

Jacobite Manchester

Many traditionally-minded Mancunians remained loyal to the exiled Stuarts over the German imports summoned by parliament. Embracing the cause of 'James III' (Latin *Jacobus*), these Jacobites would even suffer martyrdom for their 'King over the water'. Manchester folk served the Old Pretender in both the invasions of 1715 and 1745. Bonny Prince Charlie even had his HQ here from the 29 November to 10 December 1745, at a house in Market Street, known thereafter as 'the Palace'.

Most tragic of all is the story of the Syddalls, father and son, each losing his head for the legitimist cause. Tom Syddall sought to avenge his father, executed for his part in the '15, but was left defending Carlisle Castle while Prince Charles escaped over the border. Tom was hanged in London, and his severed head was set on a spike over the old Exchange, opposite the house of his grieving widow. Culloden soon ended Jacobite hopes, and the triumphant pro-government party organised a thanksgiving which ended in the trashing of the houses of the bereaved families of the rebels.

John Byrom, a prominent Manchester merchant and wit, felt a strong sentimental attachment to the Jacobites, but caution kept him from joining fully with the rebels. The ambiguities of the period are well summed up in his rhyme:

> God bless the King! God bless the Faith's Defender!
> God bless – no harm in blessing – the Pretender!
> But who Pretender is, and who is King,
> God bless us all! That's quite another thing.

The Opium Eater & the Necromancer

One of our most famous literary sons is too little known as a Mancunian. Nevertheless, author **Thomas de Quincey** was born here in Cross Street, on the 15 August 1785. The family soon moved to a more commodious home at Greenheys, and though it is hard to picture it of the modern university district now, this was then separated from the town by fields and a lonely country lane. *Confessions of an English Opium Eater* is his best memorial, and remained the chief authority on narcotics and addiction for many years. But this was all before the young Thomas when he was dipped in the font at our Saint Ann's…

Another overlooked resident is the notorious or perhaps misunderstood **Dr John Dee**, who served as Warden of the Collegiate Church from 1596 till 1609. His alchemical and occult studies might have led him to fall foul of the Church, but for the patronage of Elizabeth I. Alongside astrology, teaching navigation and promoting imperial expansion, Dee claimed to hold spiritual conferences with angels. Despite cautioning against superstition in a case of 'demonic possession' of seven local children, exotic rumours persisted. A charred 'hoofprint' on a table in Chetham's Library is said to mark his audience with the Devil.

His Welsh cousin drove seventeen cattle up to be pastured in the fields that would later form the city centre, and his son Arthur married a local girl, Isabella Prestwich. His time at Manchester would mostly be spent in tiresome legal wrangles, however, and disputes with the puritanical fellows of the college. His young wife Jane perished in the plague of 1604, along with several of their children.

This esoteric scholar inspired Shakespeare's Prospero and Marlowe's Faust, and his spell lasts to the present, inspiring Damon Albarn's eponymous opera, premiered at our 2011 International Festival.

Thomas de Quincey.

Manchester Angels

The oldest preserved artefact of Manchester (as opposed to the older Roman Mamucium) is a peculiar ancient carving in the local red Collyhurst sandstone. Found in 1871 during repairs to the stonework of the cathedral's porch, it shows a winged angel bearing a rolled scroll, most likely dating to the very earliest Norman period, if not from slightly before the 1066 Conquest. It is displayed in the cathedral and the inscription, though badly worn, is just about legible as the Latin *In manus tuas commendabo spiritum meum*, i.e. 'Into Thy Hands, O Lord, I commend my soul' from Psalm 31.

Manchester folks' spirits were sustained in later periods by another Angel, an inn on Market Street now lost, and its successor and namesake on Angel Street. Remembered in an old ballad, it appears that there was at least one young lass within who lived up to its name:

> Yes, I met a pretty young doxy, the prettiest ever I see,
> At the Angel Inn in Manchester, there is the girl for me.
> …
>
> But constant and true-hearted, love, for ever I'll remain,
> And I never will get married till my soldier comes again!

Angel Street leads us also to the Angel Meadow, where word association and tragedy have earned this former burial ground, located beside one of our worst Victorian slums, a reputation for apparitions of these celestial beings.

Future Plans

Compared to Rome, London or Moscow, Manchester is relatively young as a city. For most of its 2,000 year history it has been a regular market town, and it simply hasn't had time to catch up yet. And there is a *yet*, as Manchester is entering the twenty-first century with its eyes forward, most indicative of which are the arrival of the BBC at Salford Quays' MediaCityUK (3,000 jobs), and the grandiose plans for Manchester's eastward expansion.

The Eastlands project involves the shifting of Manchester's centre of urban gravity out from its compact nucleus, starting with the Commonwealth Games stadium in the suburb of Bradford, with much still to come. The Metrolink is expanding, bringing the conurbation back into full communication.

New trends in football have also inserted the wild-card of Gulf oil money into the equation around Sport City. The latest plans here look set to build a real foundation for the continuation of our footballing success well into the new millennium, including the building of a 'mini-stadium' in a training complex of sixteenth pitches.

A little further north, the development of Manchester Central Park, with its iconic new station and ultra-modern business and science park (involving Fujitsu and the digital media Sharp Project), is revitalising the once dilapidated A62 corridor, beginning with its state of the art station.

In the city centre, NOMA (North-Manchester) is another major new development headed by the local Cooperative Group, incorporating a landmark building shaped like a sliced egg or cone.

Things to Do

Munch on a Manchester Egg – our pickled egg + black pudding answer to the Scotch Egg – at the Castle Inn on Oldham Street.

Peep into the well in the ancient cloisters of Chetham's Library to see the fox within staring up at you!

Attend a service at the cathedral, or just inspect the hilarious carvings of rabbits roasting men or pigs playing pipes and reading books on the undersides of the misericords in the choir.

Oysters and a pint in the Shambles, in one of our two oldest public houses, the Old Wellington or Sinclair's Oyster Bar.

Swig another pint in Campaign for Real Ale approved Marble Arch pub on Rochdale Road.

If the stomach can take any more, there's always the 'All You Can Eat' option at one of the buffets in Chinatown.

Watch an outdoor film from a deckchair in Spinningfields.

Admire the Pre-Raphaelite masterpieces at the Manchester Art Gallery.

Take afternoon tea and a tour at our Victorian Town Hall.

A visit down to Salford Quays on the modern trams.

Check out the exhibitions at the Lowry Centre, climbing to the top of the unusual 'broken globe' that is the Imperial War Museum North.

Watch an opera at the Opera House, a musical comedy at the Palace Theatre, or listen to a symphony by the Hallé at the Bridgewater Hall.

Relive the Haçienda days and dance the night away with the students at Jabez Clegg nightclub, named after the eponymous character of Isabella Banks' *Manchester Man*.

You Are Now
Leaving Manchester

Captions and Credits

Page:

59. Britannia Hotel/Watt's Warehouses (Cnbrb); Arndale Centre tower seen through the big wheel; Manchester Town Hall (www.julius.tik.lt)

61. Beetham Tower; Sunlight House (left)

63. Museum (Marketing Manchester); MOSI

64-65. Lowry Centre; Greater Manchester Fire Service Museum (Marketing Manchester); Greater Manchester Museum of Transport; Tudor drinks at Ordsall Hall (Salford Museums Service)

67. Temple, Heaton Park; farm, Heaton Park

69. Cathedral Square; Saint John's Gardens

71. Goose at Bridgewater Canal; *Buddleia davidii*

73. David Livingstone (courtesy of the Library of Congress, LC-USZ62-130766)

75. NOMA; Kellogg's, Trafford Park (courtesy of Kellogg's)

77. Emmeline Pankhurst under arrest, 1914; Cobden statue, Saint Anne's Square

79. John Joule statue in the Town Hall (KaihsuTai); Dalton statue outside University

81. Frank Sidebottom mural, Oldham Street; Mark Addy pub on the Irwell

83. Courtroom capers (Greater Manchester Police); cell in Faraday Street Police Station (Greater Manchester Police)

85. Albert Square

87. White Lady of Ordsall Hall (© DMC Photographic, provided by Salford Museums Service); Ordsall Hall external (© Nick Harrison, provided by Salford Museums Service)

89. The Shambles, moved from their previous location after the IRA bomb of 1996

92-93. MCFC supporters at City of Manchester Stadium (Marketing Manchester); MUFC supporters at Old Trafford (Marketing Manchester)

95. Manchester Literature Festival 2011 (Ed Swinden at MLF); Manchester Literature Festival (MLF)

97. Ricky Hatton 2009 (SamboD); Norman Foster in Dresden, 6/11/2010 (bigbug21)

99. Herman's Hermits, 1965; The Bee Gees (NCRV)

101. Bez, 2007 (A l'origine); Morrissey (Caligvla); Noel Gallagher playing 'Champagne Supernova' (Anirudh Koul)

103. Bernard Manning (Ianmacm)

105. Running man sculpture at Sport City; Manchester Velodrome (Marketing Manchester)

107. MUFC souvenirs on sale at Ship Canal; Kippax pub, Newton Heath
109. Manchester's Baronial Hall (Chetham's Library); Hall i'th'Wood, Bolton (John Darch at geograph.co.uk); Gorton Monastery interior (Pete Birkinshaw)
110-111. Long Millgate, 1859 (Chetham's Library); Sun Inn, Poet's Corner, Long Millgate (Chetham's Library); Long Millgate; Long Millgate
113. Les Dawson as 'Ada Shufflebottom' (Terry Ravencroft); Steve Coogan in character as Pauline Calf (Martin Glyn Murray)
115. Charles Edward Stuart
117. Thomas de Quincy; Dr Dee and Edward Kelley raising a spirit (www.fromoldbooks.org)
119. Angel Stone, oldest fragment in the cathedral, late Anglo-Saxon (Manchester Cathedral)
121. BBC at MediaCityUK, Salford Quays; plans for a massive new MCFC training complex at Sport City
123. Bridgewater Hall, home of the Hallé Orchestra (Marketing Manchester); The Old Wellington Inn at the Shambles
124-125. Beetham Tower from Hulme Roundabout